CW00498194

# Brokenness
## To
## Beauty

# Five Women
# and
# Their Sons

Val Cottee

All scriptural references taken from the New International version of the bible published by Hodder and Stroughton, 2011 unless otherwise stated.

Cover designed and created with the help of Cover Creator.

# Dedication

This book is dedicated to my family whom I love so much; to past, present and future generations who have put my life into an earthly context.

# Acknowledgement

Many thanks to Michael Ross Watson, a great teacher, pastor and spiritual father, whom I have the privilege of calling a friend. His remarks in his Christmas blog 2014 started the wheels of my mind turning and from these thoughts a book was born! To my friend Paula, I say thank you again for painstakingly sifting through my work, adding the necessary comments and punctuation and putting up with my many revisions! Lastly, thanks to all my encouragers at Kerith Community Church who inspire me to keep writing and especially to all the women who have crossed my path and helped me to understand so much more of the love and the grace of God.

# Five Women and Their Sons

## Contents

# Introduction

I'm not a creative person in the accepted sense of the word. I don't knit, paint or sew if I can help it, and I often have to rely on the flair of others to help me to decorate my home and to choose colours that blend. While I have taught, both in the church and in my profession, I'm not a great speaker and sometimes struggle to find the words to express myself adequately. Yet here I am again, wanting to write the things that God has put into my head and upon my heart. He creates pictures and concepts in my imagination and I've discovered that in God there is an endless flow of resources and creativity. We are all creative, whether we realise it or not; we create an atmosphere, either positive or negative by the words we speak and the way we conduct ourselves. Should I spend the rest of my days writing, I will never exhaust the treasures found in God's Word. He will always be with me in the person of the Holy Spirit, who is the creative force in each of our lives.

Writing also brings me face to face with an awesome God who has figured so significantly, wonderfully, yet sometimes painfully in my own life and with hindsight I know that His ways are always best.

My own upbringing was sometimes lonely and somewhat Victorian and 'religious.' Everything always had to look good on the surface and anything improper or shameful was hidden. My family were very small in number and in the main were church-goers. Although I loved them dearly, we were experts in papering over the cracks of anything that might look unseemly or unpleasant to the world outside.

On Sundays we only did 'nice' things; like going to church - sometimes three times - and wearing our best clothes, which were reserved for special occasions. We were not allowed to play in the streets or go to the beach for fear of being contaminated by 'the world.' I was once rebuked by a church leader for appearing one Sunday in a trouser suit - they had just come into fashion and I felt smart! This disapproval made me feel insecure in my faith and destiny. I felt that God would only be pleased with anything that looked perfect, so I lacked any assurance of salvation, as I knew that all too often I had sinned. We did not do any work in the house apart from preparing meals and we most certainly did not shop on a Sunday; if we were short of anything we would go without.

At a later date I lodged with Christians at the beginning of my working life and we were allowed to listen to music but only of the classical genre! There were not many televisions around in people's homes in those days, but if we were among those fortunate to have one, on Sundays it would never be switched on. We could have been mistaken for Orthodox Jews trying to live out a legalistic lifestyle! Our failures and needs were never discussed in public or even in a church setting, as everything had to appear to be very respectable.

Even as a teenager I wanted to escape from this sort of lifestyle, I wanted to live in the real world with real people. I was grateful for all that I had learned about God, but saw him as a distant disciplinarian who was strongly disapproving of anything I did wrong. I longed to be loved and accepted by God for what I was, but abandoned any hope of ever pleasing him. I had little concept then of his grace and mercy.

During my days of training as a nurse and then a midwife, I began to see life in the raw; people in the towns and cities living in circumstances beyond my imagination. All dignity and pretence were stripped away, and past hurt and pain became obvious to anyone who was interested enough to enquire or listen. It was at that point that I developed a passion to help needy women, while being acutely aware of my own needs and failures.

As a married woman with children of my own, I realised all too often that life is never perfect, but God led me to a church where our imperfections were often spoken about. It was not in order to make us feel condemned, but there was a release in sharing with others and asking for their help, realising that they too had problems and failures. We would pray for one another to receive strength and the faith to believe that God would answer prayer and give us hope for the future. Eventually God gave me, along with others, opportunities to come alongside women of all ages and backgrounds and to help them in some small way to rise to their full potential in God, no matter who they were or what they had done. I heard stories that were jaw-droppingly honest and saw a desperation in women to shake off the effects of horrendous past trauma and events. I saw many women freed and delivered from the bondage of tragic and sinful circumstances, as I came to experience my own personal freedom from the sinful choices I had made. I can now pay tribute to those women who helped me to understand more of the depth of God's love and the enormity of His grace and forgiveness.

Discovering who we are and our ancestry has become a very popular pastime or hobby and is intriguing to the majority of us. We like to be able to trace and understand our roots, it gives us a sense of identity and puts our lives into some sort of context. In the pursuit of discovering our past we can find unsavoury traits and actions in the people who helped to fashion us: things to be cherished but also secrets of brokenness we would want to keep hidden. We can become deeply moved if we discover that our ancestors have suffered in any way and wish we could have changed their circumstances.

Quite recently I tried to discover something about my father's side of the family, as I never knew him or any of his relatives. He had been adopted at an early age by people who were well off financially and gave him a secure upbringing, a long way from where he would have called 'home.' I found that he was the youngest of three children and had been born in a workhouse where he was abandoned to others who would care for him. I tried to imagine what life must have been like for his biological family; they were poverty stricken and had no place to live and call their own. As I stood in that same village unable to find anyone who had known them, the tears welled up inside of me. At that moment in time I felt very close to them although they were complete strangers to me. I desperately wanted to find that they had been helped in some way. I wonder if Jesus felt the same about His ancestors!

Both Matthew and Luke, at the beginning of their gospels take care to reveal to us the detailed ancestry of Jesus. A person's family line proved their standing among God's chosen people. Luke records the names and generations back to the time of Adam, but only the male lineage is recorded, whereas Matthew starts with Abraham, the father of all Jews and records both the names of the men and the women. They are eager to show that Jesus was born of the line of Abraham and King David. Prophesies from long before were being fulfilled. God had made a covenant with his people that all the nations would be blessed by them and their offspring. How would God do this? Surely some of the men and women mentioned were not the sort of people that most of us would have chosen! Weren't they just a bunch of no–hopers? Yet we see God working in a mysterious way through the most unlikely of people.

Jesus descended from the tribe of Judah, whose mother was Tamar, a foreigner and also a seductress. Salmon was the father of Boaz whose mother was Rahab the prostitute. Boaz was the father of Obed, whose mother was Ruth, who was born in the pagan land of Moab, a land that was referred to in the Psalms as a 'wash pot,' a dirty and contaminated place. (1) Obed was the father of Jesse and Jesse the father of King David. Solomon was the son of David and Bathsheba, who had been Uriah's wife and also committed adultery. Matthew then proceeds to trace the ancestry of Jesus right down to Joseph, a carpenter and the husband of Mary, a young, peasant girl, a virgin who gave birth to Jesus, the Christ.

So we have five women; Tamar, Rahab, Ruth, Bathsheba and Mary, all very different, yet featured as being in the line of the most famous and most talked about person who ever lived: Jesus Christ, who singularly turned the world upside down, was placed in this context. Nothing was kept hidden, but would he have wanted some of those people obliterated from his past history I wonder? Would he have tried to paper over the sinful cracks of his descendants? Would he have been ashamed to have been associated with them?

Jesus was not the king that many of the Jews had been looking for. He did not have a physical kingdom in which to reign, nor did he look like a king or even act like one. He came to ordinary, simple and marginalised people; he had the common touch and he established his kingdom in the hearts and lives of those who accepted him. There was no one beyond his reach, or too sinful to be included in his family; he became known as the friend of sinners, as he dined with social outcasts and was unafraid to touch the 'unclean.' He came into the world to save lost people, not for those who felt they had no need of him and were superior to others.

Isaiah records:

*"All of us have become like one who is unclean, and all our righteous acts are like filthy rags;"*
Isaiah 64 v 6.

There is nothing we can do, to make ourselves righteous in the sight of a holy God. We cannot fix our own brokenness, it is only as we accept his Son and the sacrifice he made for us on a cross. The cross was a symbol of suffering and shame but through the suffering, death and resurrection of Jesus we can be made right with God and whole again and can reach out into a world of lost and broken people with the love, light and hope of a Saviour who died to dispel the darkness, sin and shame in all of our lives.

In this book we will look at the lives of these five woman, warts and all! Their stories are recorded in the inspired Word of God for our benefit. We can also be amazed at God's only Son coming to earth, a divinely human paradox, so that we might be included in his wonderful family and claim our new inheritance in him.

(1) Psalm 60 v 8 The Amplified Bible
Published by Zondervan

# Tamar

Genesis 38 vv 1-34

Many people say that truth is stranger than fiction. In the bible we find true stories of real people, nothing is kept hidden and with such people's lives we can all identify. Following the incident where Joseph was sold by his brothers to Midianite merchants, at Judah's suggestion, they dipped his robe in blood and returned it to their father who thought his beloved son had been eaten by wild animals. We see jealousy, envy, malice and murderous thoughts. We also see lies, deception and intense pain caused to a loving father. Jacob in his grief and distress went into mourning and would not allow anyone to comfort him. Within the story of the life and times of Joseph, another story emerges which is the story of Judah, his older brother, and a woman called Tamar.

Judah, Jacob's fourth son whose mother was Leah, was a natural leader. He was often outspoken and decisive, but his decisions were often shaped by the pressure of the moment more than his desire to cooperate with God's plan. He turned his back on his father and other brothers and went to lodge with a man called Hirah who lived in Adullam, a town south west of Jerusalem. God's plan was to keep the Israelites together in order to form a nation and to give them a sense of identity and belonging as his chosen people. He knew that if they had stayed in Egypt they would have been drawn towards worshipping other gods. While Joseph had been separated from his brothers by force, Judah chose to separate himself. He ran away from his family, his religion and his moral convictions in order to seek his fortune among ungodly people.

While away from his family and all that was familiar, he met a pagan, Canaanite woman and married her and she gave birth to three sons. In doing so, he set off a chain of sinful events. As time passed Judah found a wife for his eldest son Er, and her name was Tamar, but Er became so wicked that God had him put to death. Tamar was left alone; young, childless and a widow.

The Levirate Law was such that widows were not allowed to marry outside of the family, but one of the dead person's brothers was obligated to take her and marry her. The first son born to Tamar would carry on the name of the dead husband so that his name would not be blotted out from the nation's history. If the brother refused to marry the widow she would go to the town gate where the elders sat and they would summon the brother, reason with him and hope for a change of mind. If he persisted in not wanting to marry her, she would go to him in the presence of the elders, take off one of his sandals and spit in his face. (1)

As was their custom, Judah then commanded his second son Onan to fulfil his duty to Tamar and marry her so that she may produce offspring for her dead husband through him. Onan, realising that any son would not be exclusively his, did not relish this plan and as the bible puts it, he "spilled his semen on the ground" so that she would remain childless. He wanted all the pleasure of sex but without the responsibility. This also displeased God and Onan died as a result of his failure as a husband and father.

Tamar had two unsuccessful relationships; hope was dwindling, as she remained a childless widow. She lived in her father's house in the hope that Judah's third and last son, Shelah, would grow up and become old enough to marry her, so fulfilling his duty to her as her husband. This was her last chance, as to marry anyone outside of the family would be seen as adultery. She felt the intense pressure of knowing that the family line must not be allowed to die out, but Judah failed to keep his promise and withheld his youngest son from her. Maybe he feared for the life of his only living son, who was possibly weak or sickly, as his name is translated.

After many years of waiting and hoping for a child, which increasingly looked unlikely, Judah's wife also died and then Judah was also left alone and grief stricken. He may have been too preoccupied with his own loss to have given Tamar any further thought.

One day as he came out of mourning, he and his friend Hirah went out to the fields to a place called Timnah where his men were shearing sheep. Life had to return to some degree of normality and he decided to engage himself in work. It may have been the end of a season and a time of festivities when a great deal of food and wine was consumed. On such occasions the people would be dancing, merry and uninhibited.

When Tamar heard of his intentions she devised her own plan and took advantage of the situation. She took off her widow's clothes, covered herself with a veil to disguise her identity and sat down on the side of the road. It was customary for prostitutes to take up their positions along a road, so when Judah saw her sitting there he mistook her for a shrine prostitute and, not realising that she was his daughter-in-law, invited her to sleep with him.

Public or shrine prostitutes were common in the pagan culture of Canaan. They served the Canaanite gods and fornication was encouraged as it was thought to improve fertility in the crops and flocks. There were also private prostitutes, who were not respected and were often punished if found out.

"What will you give me to sleep with you?" Tamar asked Judah. He was rich, he could afford to pay and at first he promised a young goat from the flock. This would have provided some means for her to live on in the future, as a goat could produce offspring and she would have been sustained with milk and meat; however, in her greater and more devious plan, she asked him for a pledge until she received the goat. She wanted his seal, which was a means of his identification. A seal usually had a unique design carved in stone and was worn on a ring or around the neck of the owner; it was used by the rich and powerful people to mark clay or wax, thus authenticating legal documents. This particular seal had a cord attached which she asked for, along with the staff in his hand, so he gave them to her and slept with her and she became pregnant by him. Judah gave away his identity for a night of lust!

On leaving the place where this had happened, she took off the clothes she had disguised herself with and put back on her widow's black mourning clothes. In the meantime Judah sent his friend back to her with the promised goat, so that the pledge could be returned to him, but the friend could not find her. He looked everywhere and enquired among the people living around as to the whereabouts of what he thought was a shrine prostitute, but they knew nothing of such a woman, so he returned to Judah to report his findings.

Judah, in order to cover his tracks and to prevent himself from being a laughing stock among the people, decided to allow her to keep the pledge. He felt he had done all that was possible to find her and keep his word, but it had been without success. He decided to forget about the whole incident and move on, but we know that sin never goes away. No matter how long we try to hide our sin we know that it eventually comes to the surface. It has to be dealt with!

Three months had elapsed and life continued as normal. Judah, by this time had fully returned to his life as a shepherd and a landowner and had put the incident out of his mind. Tamar's pregnancy would not have shown at first but as time passed she decided not to hide it any longer. She spoke to others about her condition and someone was quick to make an assumption and tell Judah that she had been found guilty of prostitution. His immediate response to this disturbing news was to have her exposed publicly and then to have her burned to death. He would not risk having his daughter-in-law disgracing the family name so no mercy was to be found for her.

As she was being brought out to face her punishment she claimed to be pregnant with the man who owned the seal, cord and staff. Judah recognised his possessions and was willing to own up to his mistakes conceding that he was the one to blame. Had he experienced a change of heart? He knew that he was guilty of not honouring her in the accepted way by providing her with a husband and he had taken advantage of her because of his lust. His sinful behaviour was not compounded as he did not sleep with her again.

When the time came for her to give birth, twin boys were delivered, but she had a difficult and complicated birth as they contended with each other even before they were born. One of them put out his hand and, as he drew it back, his brother was born first. Their names were Perez and Zerah. Perez became the father of the Perezites and through him and Hezron his son and their descendants the Messiah was born. Zerah, his twin brother became the father of the Zerahites, among them was Achan whose sin at

Jericho brought about judgement on the whole nation of Israel in the time of Joshua. (2)

At first we see how quick Judah was to blame someone else for his own sin. Tamar had sinned but not out of lust, it was more about her fierce desire to bear children, and to continue the family line. In Canaanite culture this was the most important role a woman could play and the burden of childbearing was upon her. She took a huge risk, as she knew that if a wife committed adultery she could be executed.

The shrine prostitutes did not always have families of their own so were supported by the men who used their services, but their children were nobodies in society. If Tamar had become pregnant through a man outside the family, the child would not have been included as part of Judah's family but would have been a 'nobody.' She acted within the spirit of the law in wanting to provide him with a legal heir, but he had broken the law by withholding his youngest son and became immoral as a result of living among the Canaanites who worshipped other gods. Was what she did honouring to God? No! She committed the sexual sin of fornication, prostituting herself and she had taken her destiny into her own hands. Prostitution was considered to be a serious sin throughout scripture.

How then would Jesus have dealt with her, I wonder? I think he would have seen her longings, her loneliness and her pain. He would have recognised her desperation and seen that her child bearing days were running out and I believe he would have shown compassion towards her. We are given a clue as to how he might have treated her by the example of the woman caught in the act of adultery in the New Testament, a sin that cannot be committed alone! There had to be a man involved but why was only one offender brought before Jesus?

Her accusers, the Pharisees and the teachers of the law were eager to have her stoned to death, but Jesus responded by writing on the ground! He did not come to a hasty decision or give a defensive answer, and the Pharisees thought they had trapped him by finding him guilty of breaking God's holy law. I wonder if he was taking a moment to reflect upon past events, and consider how best to show mercy and grace to the sinful woman?

He disarmed her accusers by saying to them:

*"Let any one of you who is without sin, be the first to throw a stone at her."* John 8 v 7

Again we see Jesus stooping to the ground in an unhurried way and writing. He was not flustered by those who sought to catch him out and trip him up. Instead we see that one by one her accusers went away until the woman was left alone with Jesus. The man was also guilty of adultery and it would be easy for us to feel a sense of injustice and anger towards him, but he missed out on a vital encounter with Jesus, the only one who was able to bring about lasting change in his heart, so he probably continued in his sinful behaviour. Not one of us is without sin, so we cannot stand in judgement of others.

Did Jesus approve of adultery or see the woman merely as a victim? No! He called it what it was - sin, but he did not heap condemnation upon her. Condemnation brings a heaviness into our lives and a helplessness to change our ways; instead he forgave her, he let her off the hook but told her to go and leave her life of sin. His encounter with this woman was life changing for her. She deserved and expected condemnation and punishment, instead she found acceptance and forgiveness. I don't think she would ever have wanted to return to her old life. (3)

One of the most ardent followers of Jesus had been a prostitute who lived a sinful life in the town. She knew just how much she had been forgiven and as an act of worship broke a jar of expensive perfume and poured it on his feet. Her shame had been taken away, which enabled her to live a clean, wholesome and worshipful life. (4)

Jesus, the Lord of heaven and earth, who lived in glory with the Father was prepared to be mistaken for a 'nobody' in society, born into a line of sinners, so that we might become 'somebodies.' How amazing is that! We too have sinful backgrounds; we are sinners by habit and by choice, but the story of Tamar lives on to bring hope and light into the darkest of happenings. From her line a Saviour is born who was also known as a 'Lion from the tribe of Judah.' (5)

Judah, changed when he recognised his sin; not only of taking advantage of his daughter-in-law Tamar, but also of being the one to suggest that Joseph, his younger brother, should be sold into slavery in Egypt. They did not know if Joseph was alive or dead but Judah returned to his own family and offered his life as a substitute for the life of his youngest brother Benjamin, sparing their elderly father of any further grief and pain. He could not change the past but was willing to live under condemnation all the days of his life if any harm came to Benjamin when finding food in Egypt. (6)

This is one of the most moving stories told in the Old Testament and is but a glimpse of God's plan for the world. God did not withhold his only Son, but gave him willingly for us. Jesus, Judah's earthly descendant, would offer his own pure and sinless life as a substitute for us and bear the blame and punishment for all our sin on a cross.

(1) The Levirate Law. Deuteronomy 25 vv 5-10
(2) The sin of Achan. Joshua 7
(3) The woman taken in adultery. John 8 vv 1-11
(4) The sinful woman. Luke 7 vv 36-50
(5) Judah the lion Genesis 49 vv 8-10
    & Revelation 5 v 5
(6) Judah offers to take the blame Genesis 43 vv 8-9

**Something to Consider**

Are there things in your life you have tried to keep hidden? Do you feel that after reading this chapter you can bring those things into the light of a loving Saviour whose forgiveness is beyond limits?

Do you still blame others for your own sin? Are you willing, like Judah, to own up to your own mistakes? It is only as we confess our sin and repent that we can be made clean and righteous.

Does our worship reflect immense gratitude to God for his lavish forgiveness towards us?

# Rahab

Joshua 2

The years of roaming from one place to another in a desert region must have seemed endless and exhausting to the Children of Israel. Some of them had been on the move for their entire lives. They had known nothing other than living in tents, so many became used to their way of life. Some had forgotten that their forefathers had been slaves in Egypt, while others held on to the promises of God and were looking forward to putting down roots and settling somewhere safe and secure.

Joshua, who had been a leader in training under Moses, played a key role in the exodus from Egypt. He was a brilliant strategist and a field general in Israel's army. He was the only one to accompany Moses partly up the mountain when Moses received the law from God. His faithfulness, obedience and diligence was rewarded as Moses handed over the baton of leadership to him. He was to face the greatest challenge and adventure of his life and had been commissioned by God to be strong and very courageous in order to enter into the Promised Land and all that God had in store for his people. He was determined to capture his enemies and to bring the Israelites out of their wanderings in the wilderness.

As they neared the land that had been promised to them by God, he sent out two spies to secretly view the area surrounding Jericho, which was rich and fertile, but it was also a heavily fortified city. As a field general he thought he would need a plan; so he gathered as much strategic information as he could. He knew that he also required the agreement of the other leaders and of the whole camp to take the city by force. He assumed that they would be waging conventional warfare, with weapons, against their enemies. Jericho was eventually destroyed, but with hindsight we know that it was a supernatural act of God together with the obedience of the people. (1)

Forty years earlier Moses had sent out twelve spies to view the Promised Land but only Joshua and Caleb returned with an encouraging report. The other ten returned with frightening and disastrous stories. They saw that the land was good and fertile, flowing with milk and honey and had all that was promised to them, but the people in it were much stronger and more powerful. There were giants living there, so in their fear they spread gloom and discouragement among the people. They saw themselves as grasshoppers in their own eyes and this was followed by disunity, grumbling and rebellion in the camp. Fear paralyses people and because of their fear none of the people who had come out of Egypt, with the exception of Joshua and Caleb, entered into the Promised Land. They had reckoned only on what they could do, instead of what God could do through them. (2)

On this occasion Joshua sent only two spies. He remembered when he, with Caleb, had viewed the land forty years earlier, so probably chose faith filled men with good character. They entered the house of a prostitute called Rahab and stayed there. This house was built right into the city wall where she could see travellers coming in and out of the city and provided both lodging and sexual favours for them. I wonder how many marriages and families she had broken up! It was also a very vulnerable place for her to live. If the city was attacked her house would have been among the first to fall.

Rahab lived her life not only on the edge of the city but on the edge of society and was rejected by the majority because of her sinful ways. It seemed strange that the spies even entered her home, yet it was an ideal place for them to stay without too many questions being asked, as they could have been mistaken for clients. It also provided them with a quick escape route outside of the wall. More than that though, God had directed them to her house as he knew that even in her sin, Rahab's heart was open to him and he determined to use her in the victory over Jericho.

God sees into each and every heart; he knows our motives that cause us to act out our sinful desires but he determines to use the most insignificant and sinful of people. When others reject us, God takes us on! Rahab did not allow her past life to prevent her from emerging from the web of sin she had spun around her. From deep inside of her she knew that there was something far better to live for and she was ready for a new role and identity.

She must have heard stories about Israel's God from her lodgers and recognised him as all powerful and miracle-working. Stories about the Israelites had been circulating for some time in the city of Jericho, and it became evident that they were about to be invaded. The King of Jericho knew about the arrival of the spies, so stepped aside from his superiority and sent Rahab a message that she was to bring out the spies that had found lodgings in her house. In normal circumstances he would not have associated with her in any way, but fear drove him to desperation.

She acknowledged the fact that the spies had been with her, but lied about their whereabouts. She sent a message to the King saying that her visitors had left at dusk and she didn't know which way they had gone. She suggested that soldiers should go after them quickly, so that they could catch up with them and capture them.

The King's men set out in pursuit of the spies on the road towards the River Jordan and, after they left, the gates of the city were shut behind them so no one could get in or out. All the time she had been hiding them on the roof of her house. They were hidden under long stalks of flax, which had been harvested in the field and piled high on the rooftop to dry in the sun. After this the flax would probably have been made into yarn and was used for making linen cloth; another source of income for her. This was also an ideal place for her to conceal someone who did not want to be found.

Was her lie justified? Lying is sinful whichever way we look at it, but her faith drove her to conceal the truth. A familiar warfare tactic was to deceive the enemy whichever way possible, so perhaps this is what she thought she was doing. She was not a Jew, so may not have been aware of God's law, but in her mind she probably took this action against her own people to uphold a greater cause. We are not fully aware of her reasons, but under pressure this seemed to be the best solution. It would have been far easier for her to have handed them over for punishment. If she had given away their whereabouts she may well have found a greater acceptance and may even have been commended for being instrumental in their capture. We are led to believe that she was more concerned with pleasing a God that was trusted by the Israelites, than she was about pleasing the people in authority around her.

We have further evidence of her faith in God because of her words, when, before the spies had lain down to sleep for the night, she went up to the rooftop and said to them:

*"I know that the Lord has given this land to you and that a great fear of you has fallen on us, so that all who live in this country are melting in fear because of you. We have heard how the Lord dried up the water of the Red Sea for you when you came out of Egypt and what you did to Sihon and Og, the two kings of*

*the Amorites east of the Jordan, whom you completely
destroyed. When we heard of it our hearts sank and
everyone's courage failed because of you, for the
Lord your God is God in heaven above and on the
earth below."* Joshua 2 vv 9 - 11

Even though she shared the general mood of fear she
made a bold declaration of faith by a revelation from
God himself. She came from an unbelieving
background and became an idol-worshipping
prostitute but believed what many of the Israelites had
failed to grasp. She had taken a huge risk and made
herself vulnerable on account of these strangers and
she asked that in return they show mercy and
kindness to her. She asked for a sign from them that
they would spare the lives of her whole family. Her
parents were still alive and she also had brothers and
sisters who had families of their own and she pleaded
for them that they would be spared from death. The
spies gave her their assurance, that when they had
conquered the land her family would be saved.

Many would have judged Rahab for her way of life;
they would have assumed that she had no interest in a
God she barely knew, but she recognised something
that many of the Israelites did not, that God is no
ordinary God, nor is he a small god or a god made out
of hands, but that he is the all-powerful One, a
miracle-working God. She was not just concerned for
her own safety but stood in the gap and interceded for
those she loved. We can so easily judge others by
how they appear, but we never know how they got to

a place of brokenness or sin, nor do we know the condition of their hearts.

When it became safe to let the spies go and having received assurance of their kindness, she let them down by a rope from her window, which looked towards the outside of the city. She encouraged them to go to the hills so that they could hide and where their pursuers would not find them. If they remained there for three days it would give their enemies time to return to the city; they could then go on their way and complete the journey back to the camp. The oath made to her was not binding unless they saw the scarlet cord hanging from the window that had delivered them to safety, for this was a sign that her whole family had been gathered together inside the house. If any of them went out into the streets they would have risked being killed and the spies could not be held responsible. If she told anyone of their intentions they would be released from the oath. She agreed to all these conditions; she kept silent, gathered her family together and tied the scarlet cord in her window.

The scarlet cord reminds us of the night of the Passover, when the Israelites put the blood of a lamb on the door-frames of their houses and when the Lord God saw the blood he passed over them so that no destructive plague came upon them, and their first-born sons were saved. (3)

When the spies left Rahab they did as she suggested and stayed in the hills for three days. Their pursuers tried to hunt them down by searching all along the roads but could not find them. They eventually returned to Joshua and told him everything that had happened and were full of faith that God would enable them to capture the city.

*"The Lord has surely given the whole land into our hands, all the people are melting in fear because of us."* Joshua 2 v 24

The Israelites took the great and prosperous city of Jericho that was guarded by a mighty wall, but when the wall came tumbling down the home of Rahab and her family was spared. They entered into the Promised Land and God remembered Rahab because of her faith, which overcame her background and profession.

*"Now faith is confidence in what we hope for and assurance about what we do not see. This is what the ancients were commended for."* Hebrews 11 vv 1-2

God chooses to work through the very people that others reject and ordinary people can do extraordinary things. God sees beyond the dirty exterior into the heart. Rahab left her life of sin and eventually married a prince. She settled down with her husband and lived a clean and transformed life. She became the mother of Boaz, a good and upright son and she was the great, great grandmother of King David who became an ancestor of Jesus Christ.

Rahab overcame her fear, not because of who she was but who God is. She was resourceful and willing to help the people of God at great risk to herself, and is one of only two women listed in the Hall of Faith. (4)

*"By faith the prostitute Rahab, because she welcomed the spies was not killed with those who were disobedient."* Hebrews v 31

In the New Testament, James writes to the Jewish Christians who had been scattered around the Mediterranean due to the persecution of the Early Church. They had allowed their minds and, what they thought was their superior intellect, to infiltrate their original faith in God and their zeal to do his work. He reminds them that a person is justified not by faith alone but also by their actions. We know that deeds or works cannot save us, but true faith in Christ will always result in good deeds towards others.

Abraham was considered righteous because of his faith in God, followed by his actions, when he offered up his own son Isaac on the altar to God. Faith and action were working together and his faith was made complete by what he did.

*"In the same way, was not even Rahab the prostitute considered righteous for what she did when she gave lodging to the spies and sent them off in a different direction? As the body without the spirit is dead so faith without deeds is dead."* James 2 vv 25-26

Rahab was commended for putting what little she knew of God into action. Faith in God will help each one of us to overcome our fear and do the right thing irrespective of our past or rejection from others. Faith is practical, we can step out and take risks and trust in a God who comes alongside us to help us and is able to work out his long time plans and purposes even through us.

(1) The fall of Jericho Joshua 5 v 13 & Joshua 6
(2) Moses sent out spies to view
     The Promised Land. Numbers 13
(3) The Passover Exodus 12 vv 12-13
(4) The Hall of Faith Hebrews 11

## Something to Consider

Are you like some of the Israelites who became used to roaming around without being intentional about their lives? Are you content to stay well within your comfort zone or are you more of a risk-taker?

Have you got plans or dreams that remain unfulfilled?

Can you see elements in the life of Joshua that enabled him to become a leader? How can this affect your life or style of leadership?

Are you allowing fear or your past to spoil the present and the future, or, like Rahab, do you show a determination to rise above your situation?

Can you identify with the revelation that Rahab had of how mighty and powerful God is?

Rahab's faith led her to intercede on behalf of her whole family. How can she inspire us to pray for those we love?

How is your faith being put into action?

# Ruth

The book of Ruth is not just an account of one woman but of God's providential dealings in the life and sorrows of a family. It features three main characters, Ruth, Naomi and Boaz. It also highlights the little town of Bethlehem, which became a focal point in the fulfilment of the purposes and provision of God: a touching story of loyalty, friendship, love and redemption.

It all happened in the dark days of the judges when everyone did what was right in their own eyes, and pleased only themselves. Their rule was marked by lawlessness and violence. Constant turbulence and unrest had weakened Israel politically. Rampant idolatry had sapped the moral strength of the people who had once experienced the power of God when delivered from the bondage of Egypt. There was also a severe famine in the land. There were no kings to rule or prophetic voices to be heard.

Elimeleck, whose family had lived in the region of Bethlehem for generations, together with his wife Naomi and their two sons, Mahlon and Kilion, went to live in the country of Moab, east of the River Jordan and about thirty miles from Bethlehem. Why they went there is not clear and it seemed the most unlikely of places for them to go. The man, Moab, from whom the tribe had descended, was born from an incestuous relationship between Lot and one of his daughters. They oppressed Israel and there was fierce hostility between the two nations. Friendship with the Moabites was discouraged but not forbidden. Inter-marriage was against God's law and the Moabites were not allowed to worship at the Tabernacle, as they had not allowed the Children of Israel to pass through their land during the time of the Exodus.

Perhaps the famine had not taken its toll there to the same extent as in Bethlehem, so there was no risk of them starving to death; or maybe they were able to see the hills of Moab from where they were, which looked green and lush. Things often look attractive from a distance but the reality can be very different and our eyes are often drawn toward something we think might be better.

They left their homeland with such hope, but in the ten years they spent living in Moab, life had turned sour. Elimeleck died, and Naomi was left with her two sons who had married Moabite women, one named Orpah and the other Ruth. Eventually her sons also died and she was left alone, except for her daughters-in-law who were childless. I can only begin to imagine what this was like for her and how bereft and desolate she must have felt. She was in a foreign land with no husband, no children and no grandchildren. In those days, as we have seen already, there was almost nothing worse than being a widow without children; they were taken advantage of and ignored and were almost poverty stricken if there were no men in the family to protect them.

Naomi, in her hopelessness and not knowing what to do, had heard that God had once again provided food in her home town. The famine was over and she prepared to return to the only thing that was familiar to her, her home surroundings. Together with her two daughters-in-law she packed up her belongings and set out on the road back to Bethlehem, but this was not home to her daughters-in-law. Naomi encouraged them to return to their mothers' homes and to stay in Moab and eventually remarry men from their own country. At a time of great loss, we can often act like Naomi and push away what little we have left, but for her, it was also a selfless and painful gesture in order to free them from any obligation they may have felt towards her.

Orpah and Ruth were still comparatively young, and both of them, although foreigners had been good wives to her sons. She blessed them for the kindness that they had shown and prayed that they would once again find husbands to marry and have sons by them. She kissed them and wept over them before saying 'Goodbye.' At first they objected and insisted on going with her, but she knew she had nothing left to give them. Why would they want to go with her? She was too old to have another husband and well past childbearing years to produce more sons. She was convinced that God's hand had turned against her. Perhaps she felt as if God was punishing her for leaving Bethlehem, as in Moab she may have been forced to worship Chemosh, their god, and she knew that only the God of Israel could help her.

Imagine this tragic scene! These three empty women stand in the road weeping over one another. Parting can be so painful and eventually Orpah said her goodbyes and left, but Ruth refused to leave her mother-in-law. Naomi tried again to persuade her to return with her sister-in-law, but Ruth was determined not to leave Naomi alone. Instead she showed loyalty and devotion to the extreme. She said these touching words:

*"Don't urge me to leave you or to turn back from you. Where you go I will go and where you stay I will stay. Your people will be my people and your God my God. Where you die I will die, and there I will be buried. May the Lord deal with me, be it ever so severely, if even death separates you and me."*
Ruth 1 vv 16-17

She made a lifelong commitment to Naomi, and, in doing so, renounced all that she held dear in Moab and began an entirely new life. Her words must have deeply affected the older woman; so much so that she stopped urging her to return and together they completed their journey towards Bethlehem.

In those days Bethlehem was a small town and everyone knew one another. The people became excited when they heard of their arrival. They remembered Naomi and her family but on her arrival they have questions; *"Can this be Naomi?"* Why is she back in town? It was a different Naomi to the one who had left with her husband and sons. Her face and expression said it all! She left Bethlehem married and secure, she returned widowed and poor. Life seemed so full of promise then but now she wanted them to call her Mara, which meant 'bitterness.' The name Naomi, which meant 'pleasantness' didn't suit her any more.

Bethlehem is a place surrounded by many fields and olive groves. It was mainly a farming community and rich crops grew there most of the year, except for times of draught and famine. Due to the mild climate and the spring and autumn rains there were two harvests. The barley harvest occurred during the spring, just as they arrived, it was always a season of hope. Within the law, the corners of the fields were left for the poor people of the town to gather up the stalks that had been dropped, this was known as gleaning. God has always cared for the poor, and made provision for them. (1)

Naomi remembered that she had a relative on her husband's side of the family called Boaz, son of Rahab. He was prosperous and had a large piece of land on which he grew crops. Unlike his mother, he was well respected in the community but would he want anything to do with his long lost relative who was not even a blood relation? She had forsaken her home and her extended family to live in another land. Naomi was not even sure of his whereabouts, but Ruth decided that she could not stand by and watch them both starve to death. She took the initiative and took advantage of the law for the poor, to glean the left-over grain. She was not too proud to go into the fields and work all day as hard as she could. Maybe she felt that Naomi was too weak or old for such a task and she wanted to care for her.

When she arrived in the field to glean she did not know that she had chosen part of the territory belonging to Boaz. Was this a coincidence? I don't think so! God was beginning to turn the tide of their misfortune! God will always fulfil his promises, no matter what!

While she was there wanting to remain unnoticed, Boaz arrived to greet the harvesters and to pronounce a blessing upon them. It was customary to say *"The Lord be with you"* and the workers would respond, *"The Lord bless you."* Yet among all the workers in the field his eyes were drawn towards Ruth. There was something about her that caught his attention. She may well have been very attractive in appearance, but she also conducted herself in a humble and quiet way. Boaz was so intrigued by her that he enquired of the overseer to tell him more about her. He learned that she was a Moabite woman who had returned with Naomi. The overseer told his master how she happened to come into the field and how very hard she had worked all day. On hearing this Boaz approached Ruth. He was not angry with her for being a foreigner and a trespasser but encouraged her not to wander off into other fields. She was allowed to stay with the women who already worked for him and the men were instructed to look after her and to give her a drink whenever she was thirsty. Ruth was overawed by his kindness and wondered why she had found such favour with him, after all she knew her pagan background and had no right to be there, or to expect anything.

Boaz had been told about all she had done for Naomi, how she had left her own relatives and her homeland at a cost, to come to a strange place, and to live among people she did not know. He was a man who trusted a God of mercy and was perhaps reminded of his own ancestry, so saw beyond her background and believed that the God of Israel would repay her for all the kind things she had done and the sacrifices she had made.

*"May the Lord repay you for what you have done. May you be richly rewarded by the Lord, the God of Israel, under whose wings you have come to take refuge."* Ruth 2 v 12

Ruth had found refuge in Israel's God. As a hen gathers her chicks to protect them from harm, so God protects those who come to Him for safety. Jesus used this expression with great sorrow as he looked out over Jerusalem, before His death. They had not recognised who He was, nor accepted him as their Saviour and Messiah. He had longed to gather them to himself, but they were not willing to come to him. (2)

Ruth had left behind all that was familiar, but in so doing had placed herself under the protection of the only One who could help, the God of Israel, the Creator of the universe, whom she had come to recognise as the true God. If she had felt ill at ease and afraid at being discovered in a place where she had no right to be, her mind was flooded with peace by the encouraging words spoken to her by Boaz. She knew that she had no standing even with one of the servants, yet this important man not only allowed her to glean, but also invited her to eat with him and the harvesters at mealtimes: more than that, she was allowed to gather among the sheaves, the best of the crop.

After the day's work she threshed the barley and it amounted to an ephah (about 13 kilograms) and she took it back to her mother-in-law. Most workers would glean all day in the intense heat of the sun for very little, so Naomi was curious, to say the least. She questioned Ruth in order to learn how she had received such privileges, and Ruth told her how she had found favour with Boaz. Naomi, although bitter, still had an active faith in God and she spoke out a blessing towards Boaz, she is so thankful to have received his mercy and favour. She spoke of his kindness toward the living and the dead and named him as one of their guardian-redeemers.

A guardian or kinsman-redeemer was a relative, usually a brother of the dead husband, who volunteered to care for the extended family after a death. We saw this in the story of Tamar, but Boaz was thought to have been only a cousin. The law required that a widow should marry the brother in order to continue the family line, but Naomi was too old and could not have more sons. If the relative chose not to marry the widow, another relative could take his place. If no one volunteered, the widow would be left in poverty for the rest of her life.

When Naomi knew of the kindness shown towards Ruth, she felt protective of her and encouraged her to stay in his field and not to go anywhere else, in case she was harmed by the younger men who may have taken advantage of her. Ruth again became obedient to her mother-in-law and stayed until both the wheat and the barley harvests were over. During this time she lived with Naomi and they had more than enough food.

It was customary in those days for parents to find a house for their children to live in after marriage, as it is in some Mediterranean countries to this day. Naomi felt much stronger than when she had first returned to Bethlehem and felt obliged to find Ruth a home of her own and hoped that some day she would marry again.

She knew that Boaz would be winnowing barley that night along with the women who worked for him and she had a plan for Ruth, whom she had now come to regard as a daughter. She told her to wash, to put on her best perfume and to dress herself in her most beautiful clothes before going down to the threshing floor, but she was to remain unseen by Boaz. He would have been there both for security reasons and because the grain was mainly crushed at night while the harvesting took place during the light of day.

There was eating and drinking there and the wine probably put him in a good mood until he felt sleepy. When he lay down to rest Ruth was told to lie at his feet and uncover them. Ruth carried out her instructions to the detail. Had Naomi devised a seductive plan? She was asking Ruth to act in accordance with the law. It was common for a servant to lie at the master's feet and even to share some of his covering. In doing so, she was informing Boaz that she wanted him to be her guardian-redeemer. This meant that he could either find someone to marry her or marry her himself. He was probably more her father-in-law's generation rather than hers, but it was not meant to be a romantic gesture. Later, we see that they forged a deep bond of unselfish love and respect for one another. He would not have considered marrying Naomi as she was incapable of producing an heir for him.

Boaz had eaten his meal, and had drunk wine and we know that he was in good spirit, so he took a rest by a pile of grain to protect it from thieves. Ruth approached him quietly, and uncovered his feet and laid down with him. In the middle of the night something startled him and as he turned over he saw her. He was older than her and probably unwashed. He may well have been hot and sweaty from working hard well into the night, but she was younger, clean and beautiful and smelled so sweet. What man could resist her? Ruth revealed to him her identity and asked him to spread the corner of his garment over her, since he was thought to be the guardian-redeemer of her family. Did she risk an angry response? Would this gesture have annoyed Boaz? Was she asking too much or placing herself in a dangerous situation of being abused or molested by him? Instead we see that he is a man of honour and she received his blessing!

Boaz had not run after the younger women in Bethlehem whether rich or poor. Likewise Ruth had not been seen flirting with the gleaners in the fields. True love had waited for them both. She had asked much and now her loyalty, kindness and obedience to her mother-in-law was about to be rewarded. All the people in the town knew of her noble character and that Boaz would do whatever she asked of him, but there arose a problem in that he knew of a closer relative, probably a brother to Elimeleck, who would have first been obligated to protect her. This was a situation that had to be resolved legally!

He asked her to stay there for the night while he went to find the closer relative and to enquire of his intentions. No one must know that there had been a woman with him overnight because of their reputation and honour, but he did not allow her to return empty-handed. The harvest was over and the fields were empty, but before the morning he had poured six measures of barley into her shawl and she went back to the town and returned to Naomi. Naomi could not wait to hear if her plan had succeeded! She was once again the recipient of the kindness and provision of Boaz, but then they had to wait until the matter of the rightful guardian-redeemer was settled.

Boaz made his way to the town gate where, as in a courthouse, matters of this nature were disputed as we saw previously. No one could either enter or leave the town without passing through the gate. He stayed there until the rightful guardian-redeemer came along and the two of them sat down together to discuss the matter. He had ten elders of the town sitting nearby who witnessed all that was taking place; they were known as 'the quorum' required for a synagogue or for a marriage benediction. Boaz related the fact that Naomi had returned and wished to sell a piece of land that belonged to their relative Elimeleck. It was the concern of the whole community that a family be preserved from extinction, so he offered him first refusal of the land in the presence of the elders.

The rightful guardian-redeemer agreed to purchase it, but it had strings attached! He would also have been required to marry Ruth and to provide protection for Naomi. He would not have benefitted from the land personally but had to hold it in trust for any son born to Ruth. When he heard all of this he opted out of the agreement in case it endangered his own status and estate. Perhaps he already had a family of his own and the responsibility was too great for him, so he gave way to Boaz to do as he thought best. Boaz was then in a position to step into the gap. An old custom of agreement for the redemption and transferral of property to become final was that the person who had the first entitlement took off his sandal and gave it to the one who had agreed to buy it, and so the transaction became legal.

Boaz announced to all his witnesses that he would buy the property belonging to Naomi and declared his willingness to look after both Naomi and Ruth. Not only did he see this as his duty but he loved Ruth and would marry her to be with her, protect her and keep the good name of the men who had died. Elimeleck, whose name meant 'God is King' would live on in the town. The elders and all the people agreed to what had taken place, and added their desire that the women coming into his home would become like Rachel and Leah, who together built the family of Israel. God brought prosperity and blessing out of a barren and hopeless situation.

Boaz married Ruth, and made love to her, and she conceived and gave birth to a son. When the baby was born she handed him to Naomi. The women of the town gathered around her and gave thanks to God that He had given her a guardian-redeemer. With her two sons now dead Naomi had no hope of continuing her family line, but Ruth's marriage to Boaz changed everything and the son she had given birth to, brought Naomi out of her despair into a place of hope. She had seen much bitterness in her life but God had brought her back to a pleasant place. God renewed her life and sustained her in old age.

Ruth, who was born into a foreign and pagan culture and an unlikely person for God to use, had been faithful and loyal to Naomi. She had become better to her than seven sons, for having seven sons was considered to be the ultimate blessing! Naomi takes her grandson lovingly in her arms and cares for him, and some commentators suggest that she even adopted him. The women living around her spoke of Naomi's son! The woman who was broken and childless who had looked into a black hole of despair obtains an heir in the place of her dead sons. Death and loss were replaced by life, hope, vibrancy and a future.

They named the son, Obed, which meant 'a servant of the Lord' and he became the grandfather of King David and a descendant of our Saviour, Jesus.

Bethlehem, known as the 'House of Bread' became the place of provision, both physically and spiritually for Naomi and Ruth and their descendants. King David was born there and through David's line God chose to become a man, in the person of Jesus Christ, a baby born to Mary and Joseph. The stories of the angels, shepherds and the magi centre around it, and God demonstrated to all mankind that out of this little town his Son was destined to become the King over all kings.

God is the God of the second chance. He can bring prosperity out of our emptiness and despair, and repair the brokenness in our lives. We see the Lord's long-term purposes again being fulfilled, in the most unlikely of ways. Jesus is now our guardian-redeemer; He has brought us out of sin and darkness and purchased us with his own blood on a cross. The cross is now the place of provision for us and is relevant for all people everywhere and for all time.

Like Ruth, we were once strangers and foreigners to God but through His Son Jesus Christ, we are now:

*"A chosen people, a royal priesthood, a holy nation, God's special possession, that you may declare the praises of him who called you out of darkness into his wonderful light."* 1 Peter 2 v 9

(1) Gleaning Leviticus 19 v 9
(2) Jesus looks over Jerusalem Matthew 23 v 37

## Something to consider

The hills of Moab looked more attractive than the town of Bethlehem but everything turned sour.

Decisions determine our future! Have you ever been tempted to pursue something you thought looked more attractive, only to find the reality was something entirely different?

We see again and again how important names were at that time, they always had a meaning. Naomi called herself Mara, which meant 'bitterness.'

Perhaps there is an invisible name written on your forehead, a name you have called yourself. It may be a negative name like rejected, inferior, guilty or bitter? By knowing this story we see how God turns the most hopeless of situations around. He gives us a new name and if we believe, trust and work with him he will fulfil his plan in each of our lives. Ask God right now what name he would place upon your forehead?

When we know that the titles we see in 1 Peter 2 v 9 have been conferred upon us; how can this affect the way we share the good news of the gospel with others?

In what ways does Jesus compare with a Guardian or Kinsman Redeemer?

# Bathsheba

2 Samuel 11, 12, 1 Kings 2 & Psalm 51

'Unlikely' has become a keyword throughout this book and again we see Bathsheba as the unlikely link between David and his son Solomon, two of Israel's most famous kings. She became David's lover on account of his sin and later on he took her as his wife. She gave birth to a fourth son, Solomon, after her first child died. Out of the ashes of sin including adultery and murder God acted again and brought into being something good. It didn't even stop at kings but she became an ancestor of Jesus our Savour the One who came to save people from their sin.

The story of David and Bathsheba acts as a warning to us about the carelessness of harbouring sinful thoughts in our lives. It shows how sinful thoughts lead to sinful actions and then a more desperate situation arises that can affect and harm many people. We see this especially in the aftermath of adultery. Bathsheba may have been careless, to say the least, to bathe where others could see her; she was in the wrong place at the wrong time but more especially King David who should have been on the battlefield and at war with his men instead of idling his time away in his palace.

Imagine how the chain of events must have affected Bathsheba; she became unfaithful to her husband; she discovered an unwanted pregnancy; then experienced great loss in the death of her good and faithful husband followed by the death of her child. A seed of sin causes a harvest of unrighteousness. We know that in her loss David comforted her and she gave birth to other sons including Solomon, and she lived to see him accede to his father's throne.

From her life we see that our everyday choices matter to God. They prepare us for the bigger decisions that come our way. We also see further evidence of the amazing grace of God – beauty instead of ashes, the oil of joy instead of mourning and a garment of praise instead of a spirit of despair. (1) She became influential alongside her son who became known as Israel's wisest king. In the worst possible situation God is able to bring hope when we turn to Him. We have to live with the consequences of sin but His forgiveness is total.

All of this took place in Jerusalem, where she became a Queen in Israel and the Queen Mother. Yet the greater sin was that of King David, who initiated this chain of events. He was described as the man after God's own heart and God's chosen king to lead the nation. (2) If he became vulnerable to temptation, so can we. After our triumphs and successes both physically and spiritually we can find ourselves very exposed to the sins of pride and carelessness. David had just achieved a mighty military victory but in his personal life he gave way to lust and adultery.

It was springtime and a time when people were busy and kings went to war, but he remained in Jerusalem and was bored. In the spring the roads were dry making it easier for the wagons and chariots to move around, it was an optimal time to engage in battle and also to harvest the crops. The troops would be supplied with plenty of food to keep their strength up and the king would normally have been out in front leading the way.

Being idle is a dangerous place for any of us to be. Our physical environment, our relationships, our jobs, our health and our spiritual and emotional well-being all require effort.

One evening David, who had decided to take time out and with little to keep him occupied, got up from taking a rest and walked around the roof of the palace. From the rooftop he spotted a beautiful woman bathing and David is drawn towards this potentially dangerous situation. He is sexually aroused and desired to have her, so he sent one of his servants to find out all about her. The servant returns with the news that her name is Bathsheba and that she is the wife of Uriah the Hittite one of David's best men. In spite of hearing that she belonged to someone exceedingly honourable, he sent for her to be brought to him and he slept with her. She had already purified herself after her menstruation by taking a bath – a 'mikvah,' this tells us that she could not have been already pregnant.

Bathsheba was not a harlot, she came from a godly family. Her father Eliam whose name meant 'God is my kinsman' took care to choose for her a good and godly husband and he chose Uriah, whose name meant 'God is my light.' Bathsheba's name meant 'daughter of the oath' which referred back to the covenant that God made with Abraham. When summoned by the king, she could hardly refuse him as it may have meant punishment or even death for her.

After sleeping with David she returns to her own home, I wonder how she felt! Did she feel used, dirty and then cast aside? It may have been the end of the story, a fleeting affair, but eventually she discovered that she had become pregnant with his child. She knew that the child could not be her husband's child as he was away and on the battlefield so she sent a message back to David to inform him of her condition and to see what he would do. I feel sure that she experienced all kind of emotions; including fear, rejection and a deep sense of guilt. She may have pondered over her actions and regretted them deeply.

She knew David's reputation, she had trusted and admired him as her king, but he had lost his footing and became entangled by a web of deceit. He sent for her husband Uriah and tried to devise a plan for him to sleep with his own wife Bathsheba, so that the child would look as if it was his child. He put him at his ease and engaged him in conversation about the war enquiring how it was going. Uriah was not just a common soldier but one of David's most loyal men.

He had been with David since the time he sought refuge from the wrath of King Saul. In the midst of the conflict with the Ammonites, he remained on guard and slept at the door of the palace; unlike David who became careless and dropped his defences.

When David heard that he did not go home to be with his wife, he summoned him into the palace again and asked him the reason why he did not go back to Bathsheba. The most sacred Ark of the Covenant, his master and the Lord's men were camped out in open fields, which was so important to Uriah that he felt it would be wrong for him to go home. He could not afford the luxury of indulging himself; eating and drinking and sleeping with his wife while the other men were risking their very lives and had no such privileges.

David had already lost his moral and spiritual compass and sank deeper and deeper into sin, so invited Uriah to stay with him one more day. They ate and drank and David made him drunk, thinking that in his drunken state he would return to his wife and sleep with her, but again Uriah would not go home, but slept on a mat among David's servants.

David could have chosen to turn away from sin at any time, but the only man described as being a man after God's own heart, had allowed his heart to become hardened to the point where he seemed to know no limits. All his schemes had failed so he decided to involve others especially his servant, Joab. He told him to put Uriah into the front line of the battle where the fighting is fiercest and where he was certain to be killed. David had not been used to losing key men in battle as the Lord was always with him and led him to victory, but on this occasion he was greatly relieved when he learned that Uriah had been killed along with other soldiers. At last his plan had succeeded and the problem had been solved, or had it?

In the New Testament we see a warning to get rid of everything that hinders us. Sin draws us into a web of deceit, we become entangled by it and it then becomes difficult to get out of it. The writer to the Hebrews says:

*"Let us throw off everything that hinders and the sin that so easily entangles. And let us run with perseverance the race marked out for us, fixing our eyes on Jesus, the pioneer and perfecter of faith. Consider him who endured such opposition from sinners, so that you will not grow weary and lose heart."* Hebrews 12 vv 1b–3

Jesus is our supreme example of endurance and perseverance all the way to the cross. When temptation comes our way we can look at him, consider how he endured such pain and suffering and draw strength from him. He was resolute in doing the Father's will and would not be distracted. In looking at Jesus we will not grow weary of running the race that is set before us and lose heart in difficult situations. David's reaction is one of relief; he thought he had found his way out of the messy situation he got himself in but he had lost his way in the race that God had marked out for him. He had taken his eye off his calling to indulge himself in his own pleasure.

Bathsheba mourned when she heard that her husband was dead but when the time of mourning was over David brought her into his house and she became his wife. All now seemed well, but it is not one of those stories where they all lived happily ever after. David had what he wanted but we know that he was to pay a heavy price for his sin. Murder and rebellion became a constant threat in his family, and adultery was seen among his many wives and concubines. All of this happened as Nathan the prophet predicted and is a sobering reminder that our sin not only affects us but those we love and is perpetuated in the generations to come. (3)

David's response to Uriah's death seemed flippant and insensitive. On previous occasions he had grieved deeply for his enemies, like King Saul who tried many times to kill him, but he shows no grief whatsoever for Uriah who was a loyal and trusted friend and a good and strong servant. What had happened, how had this change of heart and character come about? The only way to cover his adultery was to sin again and again until it became such a pattern of behaviour that he seemed no longer to feel guilt or shame.

David had a frustrating life; he was overlooked by his father and brothers, when Samuel was looking for one to anoint as king. He lived and served under the vengeful King Saul who became so jealous of him that his life was always in grave danger. He was constantly at war winning battles and territory for God and his people, but, in a moment of weakness, he lost his self-control.

Self-control is a fruit of the Spirit's work in our lives, it grows as we resist temptation and stay close to God. We need to be on our guard and confess our sin as soon as we realise it, repent, turn away from the temptation and ask God to forgive us and cleanse us from all our wrong doing. (4) Sinful thoughts come from the enemy and our own ungodly desires. If we dwell upon them and allow them a place in our minds to grow, we are in trouble. We must reject them at the point of entry.

At some time or another we have all entertained ungodly thoughts that lead to wrong and sinful actions, and maybe all too many of us land ourselves in a mess because we have acted on them. As we confess our sinful thoughts we remain open to hearing God's voice, following Him and being filled with his Holy Spirit. How I see God's grace towards me over and over again throughout my life. There have been times when I deliberately and foolishly turned away from him to satisfy my own desires, yet he forgives and restores us when we truly repent.

If you feel disconnected to God, if he seems unreal or far away, it may just be that you are still harbouring sin in your life. You may find it difficult to forgive or let go of something that hurt you deeply, or perhaps you have never done a thorough work in repenting of your past wrong choices. The Bible is full of stories of men and women who fell into Satan's trap but were wonderfully rescued and freed by a loving God who provided a Saviour, yet to be born but was destined to be punished in our place.

Bathsheba gave birth to a son, but David's sin had displeased God so much that the son died. David had learned to live with a guilty conscience but God loved him too much to allow him to stay there. In his mercy, he had not yet finished with David but sent his prophet Nathan to expose him, and to make him acutely aware of his sin, in order to lead David to repentance.

Nathan told him a story of two men in a certain town, one was rich the other poor. The rich man had a large number of sheep and cattle while the poor man had one little lamb, which he nurtured, and it grew up with him and his children. A traveller came to the rich man but the rich man showed no hospitality towards him, instead he took the lamb from the poor man and prepared it for the stranger. On hearing this David was enraged and said that the rich man deserved death for doing such a mean and despicable thing. Nathan then said those poignant words *"You are the man!"*

Nathan reminded David of his anointing as king and how his life had been spared from the anger of Saul. God gave him a palace to live in, he gave him wives, the houses of Judah and Israel; and if all that hadn't been enough God said *"I would have given you more."* In a moment of weakness he had turned his back on a bountiful God and all he knew to be right to satisfy his own lust. He had stolen Uriah's wife and had him struck down and killed, therefore God proclaimed judgment on his house and his descendants.

David had to be brought back to his senses and realise the gravity of his sin. Nathan prophesied that God had taken away his sin and he would not die, but his son would. The son became ill and David pleaded for the child, he fasted and lay prostrate on the ground interceding for him, but after seven days the child died. When David heard that his prayers had not been answered in the way he had hoped, he got up, washed himself, put on clean clothes and lotion and went into the house of the Lord and worshipped. After this he ate the food that had been brought to him.

If David had known the pain that was to come about as a result of his sin he may not have wandered down that road in the first place. He was quick to see the sin in others while overlooking his own sin. Although David was truly sorry for his actions he had to live with the consequences. Sin has to be judged by God! It cannot be overlooked and with hindsight we now know that the greatest judgment of all fell on Jesus, who came from the line of David and is included in his descendants. The judgement was not on Bathsheba or on her first child but on his father David. If the child had survived, God's name would have been dishonoured by Israel's pagan neighbours.

God had to act out his judgement in the tragic loss of a baby in order to save a whole nation. Similarly God acted out his judgement in the death of his own dear Son at a place called Calvary to save the whole world.

David did not continue sinning but could not negate what had taken place. He speaks of a broken spirit and a contrite heart that God would not despise. (5) In God's lavish and amazing grace he gave David a fresh start and Solomon – whose name meant 'peace' - was eventually born to Bathsheba. He was their fourth son so several years had passed and it is quite possible that Bathsheba had remained in mourning for her first son until that time. We know that David comforted her, but more than that the Lord loved Solomon and chose him to be the future king.

There was a double blessing in store for her, as Nathan, their third son, was a direct descendant of Mary the mother of Jesus, while Joseph, Mary's husband, descended from the line of Solomon. I wonder if Nathan, their son, was named after Nathan, the prophet who spoke truth into their lives, which led them to repentance. He had been God's messenger of hope.

As we have seen already, God's plans and purposes prevail. Solomon became the wisest king on earth and in the years to come God knew that out of all this terrible and sinful turmoil his own precious Son would be born. He would live a worthy and sinless life, more honourable even than the life of Uriah.

David had sunk to the depths only to find that after much soul searching and agony of spirit, he received the mercy and forgiveness of a loving God.

*"As far as the east is from the west, so far has he removed our transgressions from us"*
Psalm 103 v 12

The east never meets the west and because God is omnipotent he can never forget, instead he chooses not to remember. God is more committed to forgiving than we are to seeking forgiveness.

*"For God so loved the world that He gave His one and only Son that whoever believes in Him shall not perish but have eternal life. For God did not send his Son into the world to condemn the world but to save the world through him."* John 3 vv 16-17.

Bathsheba lived to see David, her husband die and her son Solomon became the King of Israel. David had been chosen by God to be a warrior king so was not permitted to build the temple at Jerusalem. The temple was built under the reign of Solomon and even to this day the Jews consider the remains of Solomon's temple to be the most holy place on earth.

Bathsheba reigned alongside her son and tried unsuccessfully to keep peace between the brothers. Yet God had promised that through the union of David and Bathsheba and their descendants the Prince of Peace would be born, the one who is able to bring peace with God and the peace of God in the midst of our strife, anxiety, fear and confusion.

The prophet Isaiah said:

> *"For to us a child is born, to us a son is given, and the government will be upon his shoulders. And he will be called Wonderful Counsellor, Mighty God, Everlasting Father, Prince of Peace. Of the greatness of his government and peace there will be no end. He will reign on David's throne and over his kingdom, establishing it and upholding it with justice and righteousness from that time on and forever. The zeal of the Lord Almighty will accomplish this."*
> Isaiah 9 vv 6

(1) Beauty for ashes! Isaiah 61 v 3
(2) 1 Samuel 13 v 14 & Acts 13 v 22
(3) The second commandment  Exodus 20 vv 4-6
(4) Confession, repentance and freedom1 John 1 v 9
(5) A broken spirit and a contrite heart Psalm 51 v 17

## Something to Consider

Can you remember a time when you gave in to temptation only to have regrets soon after?

Having lived with the consequences of sin, does this affect your way of life for the future?

Have you considered why Jesus had to die? He died as though he was the guilty one so that our guilt could be removed.

David's prayers were not answered in the way he had hoped for; he got up, washed himself, put on clean clothes and went into the house of the Lord and worshipped. How do these actions speak to us?

Is there a present turmoil in your life where you need to know God's special brand of peace?

*"Do not be anxious about anything, but in everything, by prayer and petition, with thanksgiving, present your requests to God. And the peace of God that passes all understanding, will guard your hearts and your minds in Christ Jesus."* Philippians 4 vv 6-7

Self-control is a fruit of the Spirit. How can we allow this and other fruit to develop in our lives?
See Galatians 5 vv 13-26

# Mary the Virgin

Matthew 1&2, Luke 1&2, John 2 v 5,
Mark 3 vv 31-35, John 19 vv 25-27,
& Acts 1 v 14

There are many Marys mentioned in the bible but this chapter is about Mary the virgin who became the mother of Jesus. Although she was a good and clean living girl she was another unlikely person to be used by God in such a significant way. She was very young, thought to have been between twelve and fourteen years old, and engaged to a carpenter named Joseph. She must have been looking forward to the day when she would settle down and have her own family with Joseph, but her life was about to change forever.

Sexual purity was enormously valued among the Jews and it was necessary for a woman always to belong to somebody. A marriage would have been arranged for Mary, at a very early age, to someone the parents considered to be suitable and both families had to agree to the union. Following this, a public announcement was made and they then became pledged to marry, in other words, they belonged to each other. This relationship was legally binding and could only be broken by death or divorce. She would have stayed with her parents and under their protection until after the wedding, when she would then move in with her new husband and they would live together. When Joseph heard the news that Mary was pregnant, his world was shattered. He was bitterly disappointed and felt betrayed by his bride to be.

Joseph was a righteous man and even in his disappointment and confusion he did not want to expose Mary to public shame. In their culture any shame brought upon the woman would also affect the man. To defend his own honour he would have to accuse her in a court of law, which would have resulted in a very public divorce and severe punishment for Mary, even to the point of her being stoned to death. Instead he planned to privately divorce her, but there would always have been a hint of suspicion around him that he may have been the father. In his dilemma of not knowing which course to take, God intervened by sending his messenger in the form of an angel. God had a third option which he had not even considered and demanded an even deeper commitment from Joseph. He must take Mary home as his wife. Both the mother and child then would be under his protection and, when naming the child, it signified a formal adoption of the baby Jesus.

Mary was thought to have been of little significance in a culture hostile to women. Both she and Joseph were very poor. There had been 400 years of silence from heaven, with no prophets around to bring God's word to the people. Nazareth was known as a place polluted by non-Jews and was miles away from the temple at Jerusalem, the all-important place of worship for the Jews.

"A nobody girl, in a nobody town at a time when Jewish history appeared to be going nowhere, at a time when nothing was happening" (1)

"But God!" Those two little words bring a wealth of meaning to a Christian. When all looks dark and hopeless, God wonderfully intervenes and causes something good, positive and productive to emerge from the desert experiences of our lives, as we see over and over again.

Motherhood is both fulfilling and joyful as many of us know, but it can also be costly and painful at times. All of these things were accentuated in the life of Mary the Mother of Jesus. She saw him as a tiny helpless baby wrapped in swaddling clothes and nurtured him when he was very young. She was frustrated and anxious when they lost him in the temple for three days when he was only twelve years old. She witnessed the joy and pain of his life and ministry, the demands that were made upon him and equally the rejection he received when he moved out of their family home to fulfil the will of God and do his work. Ultimately she witnessed his excruciatingly painful death on a cross. Nothing and no one could have prepared her for this! Some may have already experienced the great and tragic loss of a child and know how that feels and for others of us it must be one of our greatest fears.

The angel's news was both puzzling and frightening for her. How could she possibly become the mother of the promised Messiah? Yet in her confusion she became an obedient servant. Prophecies from long ago were still spoken about among the believers, but many had given up on them, as the wait had been too long. As in the present day, most people lived in a 'now' culture of greed, violence and rebellion. They were constantly threatened by Roman rule and law and were hoping for a king to come, someone strong in battle who would deliver them and establish a new kingdom of freedom and power over their enemies.

Mary had no pre-conceived ideas of what the Messiah might look like and even though she had been greatly troubled by the angel's words, she had a tender and believing heart, open to whatever God said and however He would act. When she chose to obey God she was risking her reputation and, unless Joseph agreed to marry her, she would probably have remained unmarried for the rest of her life. If her parents rejected her she would have been forced to beg on the streets. She even risked others thinking she was deluded or crazy, having imagined that God had spoken to her.

We read that the Holy Spirit came upon her and the power of the Most High overshadowed her. Although she became obedient, this was God's work in her life; the sovereignty of God together with human responsibility. Her name is highly revered among many, particularly Roman Catholics, but she was only human and the conception was entirely the work of the Holy Spirit in her life.

Like most other women, Mary needed a confidant; an encourager and she found support in her cousin Elizabeth. They had much in common; they were both aware that God had again intervened in the history of their nation and they, in their humble state, had been significantly chosen to bring about the purposes of God. They were both expecting a son, which had come about supernaturally.

Mary was a reflective girl who pondered things in her heart; she knew the scriptures and treasured them. She was a believer and a worshipper and she also became prophetic, speaking out what we now know as the Magnificat. (2) Led by the Holy Spirit, she declared that because of this child yet to be born, all generations would call her blessed and that God, the Mighty One had done great things. He had championed the poor and had remembered Abraham and his descendants in His mercy. (3)

Circumcision was an important event in the life of all Jewish baby boys. God had commanded it when he was beginning to form a holy nation. (4) Eight days following the birth, family and friends would gather to attend the ceremony performed by the Jewish Rabbi. This was the time when the baby was named. Names were very important to the Jews as we have seen already. He was not named after Joseph his earthly father but they named him Jesus, as the angel had told them, which in Hebrew was 'Yeshua' or 'Joshua' which meant 'Saviour of the people.'

One month after the birth was the time of Purification according to the Law of Moses. Up to that time Mary would have been ceremonially unclean and unable even to enter the temple. (5) This ceremony included the redeeming or buying back the child from God by making an offering. A child's parents would usually bring a lamb for the burnt offering and a dove and pigeon for a sin offering, but a lamb was too expensive to be bought by Mary and Joseph, instead they brought the offering of poor people, which was two doves and a pigeon. There were no exceptions to the law, not even for the Son of God and Jesus said at a later time that he had not come to destroy the law but to fulfil it. (6)

Even though everything was done in a proper way according to the Law of Moses, we see yet again God's intervention in the midst of all the ritual. An old man called Simeon who was good and devout, had longed to see the consolation of Israel and, although the Holy Spirit had not yet been given freely to all believers, we know that the Spirit was upon him to prophesy. He recognised that this was the long awaited Messiah and God sent the third member of the Trinity, his Holy Spirit to be a witness to all that was taking place and to bring revelation to the people. Mary had previously thought that her baby had been sent to save the nation of Israel but Simeon said that He would be a light to the entire world.

*"A light for revelation to the Gentiles and for glory to your people Israel"* Luke 2 v 32

Mary and Joseph marvelled at this, as they realised that their little son, would be even mightier than they had dared to imagine, he had been born to save the world! Yet here in Simeon's prophecy we see a solemn warning to Israel, that the nation would both rise and fall because of Jesus. Some would joyfully accept Him while others would totally reject him. We know that many Jews today have not accepted that he was the promised Messiah and are still waiting and living under the Old Covenant. The whole nation has lived through conflict and persecution for centuries. To Mary, Simeon said "And a sword will pierce your own soul too," her heartache had begun! I believe there was great tenderness in his voice as he spoke to her but his words penetrated her whole being.

Anna was a very old and devout lady who had never left the temple since being widowed eight years after her marriage, but worshipped day and night, fasting and praying in the temple. At that moment she came to them and blessed them. She gave thanks to God that her eyes had seen something she had waited her whole life to see. Yes, Mary and Joseph had done everything the law had demanded of them but God sent His Holy Spirit and two elderly and godly people to speak his heart into their lives.

We are not told the exact timescale of events, but we know that Jesus was born in Bethlehem, and in order to escape the wrath of Herod who wanted to kill him, they took refuge in Egypt. Eventually they returned to their own town of Nazareth in Galilee where Jesus grew up and we read *"the grace of God was upon Him."*

The main part of the ministry of Jesus was conducted in Capernaum, as in Nazareth he performed fewer miracles because of their unbelief. Perhaps they had become over familiar with the carpenter's son they had grown up with and there were those who said, *"Can anything good come out of Nazareth?"* When Nathaniel was called to follow Jesus, he spoke these very words. He had to be convinced that Jesus was not just the son of Joseph, but also the Son of God. (7)

It is thought, by the time Jesus was thirty years old, that Joseph may have died, as there is no further mention of him. In their culture it was unusual for a man to leave his parents' home, so Mary and his brothers trudged behind him almost everywhere he went to keep contact with him.

We see Mary's concern at the marriage in Cana of Galilee; the wine had run out and she was embarrassed for the host. Weddings in those days were often a week long and the whole village would be invited, along with Jesus, his mother and brothers. Showing hospitality to others was all-important to the Jews, but was she asking him to do the miraculous I wonder, or merely deferring to him as her eldest son and asking for his help?

We also see her concern for him as he gave himself completely to those who sought his help. So insistent was the crowd, so intense was their needs that he taught the multitudes and fed them; he healed the sick and performed many other signs and wonders. Perhaps she wanted to take him home for some rest and relaxation as a good mother would. Jesus was not denying his earthly family but was preparing them for a necessary and gradual separation, paving the way for a new spiritual family to emerge. This new family would be made up of those who believed in him and who did the will of God. These same people would be his brothers, sisters and mothers. How difficult it must have been for her to stand back, as he became the property of everyone, rather than belonging exclusively to her.

Jesus had not abandoned Mary, nor had he stopped loving her! We see a very poignant scene at his death. Mary stood near him at the foot of the cross. If the sword that Simeon had spoken of hadn't already pierced her soul, it did then! Her grief must have been overwhelming, but Jesus looked down from his agony into the crowd; his eyes searched for his mother and he is concerned for her wellbeing. Many had forsaken him during his trial but she remained steadfast to the bitter end. He sees John, his true friend and the disciple who was often described as the *"one whom Jesus loved"* also standing there and he committed her into his care and we know that John eventually took her into his own home. Why didn't Jesus ask his brothers to care for her I wonder? Maybe at that moment in time they were not present with him nor even true believers. (8) What we do know is that those who shared in His death at the foot of the cross are those who really loved Him.

After the death, resurrection and ascension of Jesus from the Mount of Olives, Mary remained close to the other believers. She gazed intently and longingly into the sky as he was leaving them and there appeared two angels. She believed in angels and is perhaps reminded again of his birth. Angels speak encouragement to believers and on this occasion said:

*"This same Jesus who has been taken from you into heaven will come back in the same way you have seen him go into heaven."* Acts 1 v 11

All is not lost! He is coming back and one day she will see him again. She was among those who returned to Jerusalem to the upper room where they constantly prayed and waited for the Holy Spirit, whom Jesus had promised to send, and where God visited them spectacularly with His presence.

Not only is this Mary's story, but it continues to be the story of God's amazing intervention in the lives of ordinary people who dare to believe that he is the true Messiah and the Saviour of the world.

(1) A quote from J John's Christmas messages
(2) The Magnificat  Luke 1 vv 46-55
(3) God's promise to Abraham and his descendants  Gen 22 vv16-18
(4) The covenant of circumcision Gen 17 4-14
(5) Redemption of the firstborn son
(6) Numbers 18 vv 15-16
(7) Jesus came to fulfil the law Matthew 5 v 17
(8) The call of Nathaniel John 1 vv 45-50
(9) His own brothers did not believe in him John 7 v 5

**Something to consider**

Has God ever asked you to do something far bigger than you imagined? How did you proceed to act upon what you thought he might be asking of you?

What have been the joys and pain of parenthood for you? Have you a close friend or friends you can share with and pray for your family?

If you have no children of your own, are there children in your life you can support and for whom you can pray?

Jesus was born because of a supernatural event, but every baby is a miracle. David his ancestor and also a psalmist writes:

*"For you created my inmost being; you knit me together in my mother's womb. I praise you for I am fearfully and wonderfully made."* Psalm 139 vv13-14

How do these words speak to you?

# Jesus Son of God

So far we have only considered the earthly story of Jesus, as the son of Mary, a descendant of the line of Tamar, Rahab, Ruth and Bathsheba, but above all we must not forget that he had a heavenly story. We remember his birth each Christmas when he is depicted as the baby in a manger; but this tiny, helpless baby grew and lived an amazing life. He died a unique death and ascended into heaven. One day 'Great David's greater Son' will return in all his glory as the King of Kings and Lord of Lords and will judge both the living and the dead. (1)

At the very beginning of all things, he was in community with God the Father and the Holy Spirit. One in three and three in one, inextricably linked. Essentially he was God who became flesh in the person of his Son to live among us. The conception and birth of Jesus was a supernatural event beyond our own understanding or reasoning, but we do know that He was born of a virgin yet conceived by the Holy Spirit.

When the angel came to Mary, he said to her:

*"You will conceive and give birth to a son and you are to call him Jesus. He will be great and will be called the Son of the Most High.  The Lord God will give him the throne of his father David, and he will*

*reign over Jacob's descendants forever; his kingdom will never end"* Luke 1 vv 30-33

When Mary asked how this could happen. The angel continued:

*"The Holy Spirit will come upon you, and the power of the Most High will overshadow you. So the holy one to be born will be called the Son of God"*
Luke 1 v 35.

Micah prophesied centuries before:

*"But you Bethlehem Ephrathah, though you are small among the clans of Judah, out of you will come for me, one who will be ruler over Israel, whose origins are from old, from ancient times"* Micah 5 v 2

His natural birth took place in Bethlehem which is now a place torn apart by factions and political unrest. He grew up in Nazareth to be a carpenter like Joseph. His earthly ancestors, parents, place of birth and home town gave him an earthly context, but he also pre-existed with God before time began.

Jesus was born of a virgin to be free from the sin that entered the world through Adam. Adam, the first man was created sinless but because of pride and disobedience he became separated from God. Jesus, who is described as 'the second Adam' and a 'life giving Spirit' chose to obey God and to face the consequences of sin on our behalf. (2) He was born of a woman so took on human nature, but he was also the Son of God whose nature was divine. He wasn't partly man and partly God but fully man and fully God.

Because of his humanity, he understands us, our joys but also our troubles and trials. He walked through the same difficulties and emotions that we experience in our day-to-day lives. He knew temptation, rejection and suffering more than anyone who ever lived; but, because he is also God, he has the divine power to do something about it. God knew that we were helpless to save ourselves and to live an obedient life, so Jesus came to seek and to save all who were lost and to give us new life. He has made it possible for us to approach the Father with confidence in knowing that we can receive his grace and mercy and that he will help us in our times of need, distress, confusion and pain. (3)

Unlike Matthew and Luke, John makes no mention of his earthly genealogy but begins his gospel with a bold statement:

*"In the beginning was the Word and the Word was with God and the Word was God. He was with God in the beginning. Through him all things were made; without him nothing was made that has been made. In him was life and the life was the light of all mankind. The light shines in the darkness and the darkness has not overcome it."*
John 1 vv 1-5

John felt that his mission was primarily to portray Jesus as the unique and special Son of God. His identity is central to our faith! Most people would say that Jesus was a good man or even a prophet but deny the fact that he is God's Son and one in essence with God. What Jesus taught; the way he related to ordinary people and the miracles he performed came about because of his identity. He lived fully as a man, but he is also the Creator of all things and the source of eternal life.

'The Word' was a term used by theologians and philosophers, both Jews and Greeks, it meant an 'agent of creation' and was used for the God of Israel alone, rather than all the Greek gods who were worshipped at that time, but John used this term to refer to Jesus. John had lived with him, followed and loved him, yet he also received the revelation that he was indeed God in person. For him to have used 'The Word' to describe Jesus was none other than blasphemy to the Jews and to the Greeks it was unthinkable. They were scholars and to them the Word becoming flesh made no sense whatsoever. To those of us who believe that Jesus is The Word, it is good news indeed and on that premise John based his whole gospel.

The apostle Paul also wanted to emphasise his identity as God's Son. In his letter to the Colossians he wrote:

*"The Son is the image of the invisible God, the firstborn over all creation. For in him all things were*

*created, things in heaven and things on earth, visible and invisible, whether thrones or powers or rulers or authorities; all things have been created through him and for him. He is before all things, and in him all things hold together."* Colossians 1 vv 15-17

In Colossae there were many false teachers, Gnostics and heretics who claimed to be all knowing. They believed that the created world or matter, was evil and was totally separate from, and in opposition to the world of the spirit. They believed that the supreme God dwelt in unapproachable splendour and an inferior being created the physical world. This led to a depreciation of the life, death and resurrection of Jesus. They believed that salvation came about by self-realisation rather than by deliverance from sin. (4) This belief is held by many of the present day cults and is a perversion of Christianity. They believed that people could find God by their own special, spiritual and superior knowledge; whereas Paul proclaimed that the way of salvation was through Jesus Christ alone.

The Jews accepted the Old Testament and the many ways throughout history that God had tried to reach his people, but, except for those who had a revelation of his identity, they rejected Jesus as their Messiah.

John the Baptist was a believing Jew, who was sent to herald the coming of Jesus. He knew his true identity. Even as an unborn baby he leapt in his mother's womb when the birth of Jesus was announced. Not only was he John's earthly cousin, but he was God's only Son and it was this message he declared to the crowds:

*"John testified concerning him. He cried out, saying, 'This is the one I spoke about when I said, "He who comes after me has surpassed me because he was before me."* John 1 v 15

Jesus himself said:

*"Before Abraham was, I am."* John 8 v 58

This was the most radical statement the people had ever heard, as God used the "I am" to refer only to himself, it was a sacred title, so they tried to stone Jesus for blasphemy.

Jesus often had to comfort and reassure his disciples, when they had lost sight of their commission or were overwhelmed by doubt about his identity. Thomas did not always understand the ways of Jesus, who he was, or where he was leading the disciples.

Jesus said to him:

*"I am the way and the truth and the life. No one comes to the Father except though me. If you really know me you will know my Father as well. From now on you do know him and have seen him"*
John 14 vv 6-7

Philip wanted to see the Father to be fully satisfied of his identity but Jesus said:

*"Don't you know me, Philip, even after I have been among you for such a long time? Anyone who has seen me has seen the Father. How can you say 'Show us the Father?' Don't you believe that I am in the Father and the Father is in me? The words I say to you I do not speak on my own authority. Rather it is the Father living in me, who is doing his work. Believe me when I say that I am in the Father and the Father is in me."* John 14 vv 9-11

Both Thomas and Philip had been his constant companions. They had seen the miracles performed by him; the sick were healed, the blind received their sight, lepers were cleansed, the lame walked and there were many other signs and wonders, yet they still sought reassurance from Jesus, that he was truly God.

Jesus never heaps condemnation on us when we have doubts; though maybe he is saddened by them at times. Accepting who he is, is a step of faith and faith goes hand in hand with revelation. As we accept his identity he gives us more and more revelation of who he is and no matter how much we think we know him there is always so much more to know.

*"The Word became flesh and made his dwelling among us. We have seen his glory, the glory of the One and only, who came from the Father, full of grace and truth."* John 1 v 14

Three disciples, Peter, James and John, caught a glimpse of his glory when Jesus was here on earth, at the time of his transfiguration on the mountain. Paul also experienced the *'light of his glory'* on the road to Damascus at his conversion. Many times John the apostle, towards the end of his life, saw his glory in visions when he was exiled on the Isle of Patmos. (5)

Yet God is not only a holy and awesome God but also a loving Father, and when his Son was here on earth we saw that he intervened many times and used terms of endearment and affirmation towards him. As Jesus was baptised in the waters of the River Jordan, a voice from heaven said:

> *"This is my Son whom I love, with him I am well pleased."* Matthew 3 v 17

God, the proud Father, delighted in his Son Jesus, and spoke the same words when they were enveloped in a bright cloud on the mountain of transfiguration.

God, the omnipotent, divine, Creator of the universe, came to earth to initiate a rescue plan for us. Before Jesus came to earth, men and women could only know God in part but now we can fully know him, and the more we meditate on who he is, the more amazed we will be at the sacrifice he made because of his love for each one of us.

"We should treasure Jesus' divinity because it is only through his divinity that Christ is able to live for us and die on behalf of all of us. Jesus himself, therefore is a paradox – he cannot be reduced to fit our thinking. Knowing him means having our assumptions and misconceptions reinstalled, revised and redeemed." (6)

There are no words of mine that could clarify the pre-existence of Jesus, and I am completely out of my depth to do justice to his identity in God. There are no comparisons to be made, and no other examples to be given as he was and is God's one and only Son. I can only draw from what is recorded in God's Word and is given to us in the form of Holy Spirit inspired scripture.

Perhaps Jesus himself would wrap it all up by saying:

*"I am the Alpha and the Omega, the First and the Last, the Beginning and the End."* Revelation 22 v13

(1)  2 Timothy 4 v 1
(2)  1 Corinthians 15 vv 45-47
(3)  Hebrews 4, emphasises both the humanity and divinity of Christ.
(4)  The Illustrated Bible Dictionary, Intervarsity Press, Published by Hodder and Stroughton 1980
(5)  Mark 9 v2ff; Acts 9 vv 4-5; Revelation 1 vv 12-13, and 18 vv 11-12
(6)  Krish Kandiah from his book Paradoxology, Published by Hodder & Stroughton 2014

**Something to consider**

Has it made a difference to you and your prayer life that Jesus became a man with all the sufferings and temptations that we experience?

Jesus makes the claim of being one with God in the person of his Son. Is this something that you have thought about? Is he who he says he is, or is he at best deluded or at worst an evil impersonator? What is your response?

How does the divinity of Jesus make it possible for us to live a more productive life?

# Sons and Daughters!

The word 'belonging' conjures up so many warm and positive feelings of being part of something or connected to someone. The truth is we all want to belong to someone special, to belong to a family, to an organisation or a group. We were not made to go it alone. Even Adam felt incomplete without Eve, although God had placed him in a perfect environment, with everything he could have wanted. God saw that for him to be complete he had to have a companion. All of creation was good and satisfactory up to that point, but one thing was missing and he saw that it was not good. (1)

There are those who may feel threatened to have belonged to someone cruel or abusive, they longed for love but instead found fear, insecurity and danger. Maybe you feel trapped in a situation or by a person or persons and long to be free.

David, although he had a large biological family seemed to express bereft feelings and a longing to be accepted in many of his psalms.

"Though my mother and father forsake me, the Lord will receive me." Psalm 27 v 10

Some may have been rejected by their parents or experienced the loss of a mother or a father at an early age. We live in days when families are fragmented and separated because of strife, faith, distance, illness or other issues.

Again David writes that God would be:

*"A father to the fatherless"* Psalm 68 v 5

This has been my testimony! Even though I never remember sitting on my father's lap or being loved by him, God came to my rescue, he cared for me and gave me a family, his family. It is such good news that we can all now belong to a dynamic family, to a living God through his Son, Jesus Christ; and can know love and security in him without fear of abuse or rejection in any shape or form.

John writes at the beginning of his gospel:

*"To all who received him, to those who believed in his name, he gave the right to become children of God – children born not of natural descent nor of human decision or a husband's will but born of God."* John 1 vv 12-13

To the Christians in Corinth and Rome, Paul writes;

*"I will be a father to you and you will be my sons and daughters, says the Lord Almighty."*
2 Corinthians 6 v 18

*"So my brothers, you also died to the law through the body of Christ that you might belong to another, to him who was raised from the dead so that we might bear fruit to God."* Romans 7 v 4

God meant for us primarily to belong to him. You may be living many miles from your natural family, but in Christ we become members of his family, and find that we have brothers and sisters wherever there are true believers. We can know that instant connection, because Jesus has already paved the way for his new family to emerge as he demonstrated during the time of his ministry here on earth. His new family includes all those who believe in him, accept him as their Saviour and obey God.

How many of us, I wonder, have found that spiritual ties can often be as strong, if not stronger than natural or physical ties? Until I was knitted into a church, I felt lost in a place called Bracknell. I knew no one outside of my natural immediate family. Since then the bonds that have been forged with many people in my Christian community will never be broken, not even in eternity. God has now given me not only a wonderful biological family but also an amazing spiritual family.

An ideal family look out for each other, they have different roles and responsibilities but they are united in purpose. When we are born again everything is new, we have security and new desires and plans.

*"Therefore if anyone is in Christ he is a new creation the old has gone the new has come!"*
2 Corinthians 5 v 17

We are not just being made better or trying hard to turn over a new leaf but what was dead in us becomes alive. Sometimes we live as if this was not the case, but I believe that God would have us grasp our new identity and live out a transformed life by his grace and the power that is at work within us. It is not just a passive existence and Paul encourages us to put on the new self like a garment, as we are now created to be like God in true righteousness and holiness. (2)

I love new clothes especially if I can buy them in the sale at a bargain price! The truth is, I have plenty of clothes but I often reach into my wardrobe for that old familiar thing. It may be a bit drab or shabby but I feel comfortable in it and I'm reluctant to throw it away. God has given us new clothes to wear and not even at a sale price, but he offers them freely. They have been bought and paid for by his precious blood; we only have to put them on! We need to be more ruthless and get rid of our old clothes; those old sinful patterns of behaviour and the negative thoughts that enter our heads. Why do we often live and look like orphans, when we can live as children of the living God?

Perhaps like Naomi, when she changed her name to Mara, we are still wearing a negative name and an old mind-set. God has given to us a new name – an everlasting name that will not be cut off. (3)

Jesus had planned not to leave us as orphans but He promised to come to us and live not only with us but in us by his Holy Spirit. (4) We are no longer 'nobodies' but we belong to a wonderful family and have the rights and privileges of sons and daughters.

As Christians we have been given a new inheritance. The Holy Spirit has been given to us as a down payment and confirms to us that we are now God's children. It is a taste of what we will experience in heaven. (5)

The Jews looked to an inheritance in the Promised Land of Canaan. Our inheritance came about by the death and resurrection of Jesus Christ and he has gone ahead of us to prepare a place where we will live with him forever. A brand new home, a mansion!

When Jesus spoke to his disciples about leaving them, they felt frightened and anxious. They couldn't imagine what life would be like without him. Jesus told them that it was good for him to go away as he would send someone else in his likeness and character. He would be called the Holy Spirit; someone who would lead them into all truth. We who have followed on need not to give way to fear but can understand and experience the same rights and privileges through the Holy Spirit today. The Holy Spirit is our teacher, the code breaker to the mysteries that are hidden for us in Christ. (6)

*"For you did not receive a spirit that makes you a slave again to fear, but you received the Spirit of sonship, and by him we cry 'Abba, Father.' The Spirit himself testifies with our spirit that we are God's children. Now if we are God's children then we are heirs- heirs of God and co-heirs with Christ"*
Romans 8 vv 15-17

Paul, a man who had persecuted the early Christian Church, by hunting down its members and having them put to death, claims that we are not only sons and daughters but heirs. He knew what it was like to live on the edge of society and to be devoted to an evil cause, but his Damascus Road conversion changed everything. He knew that he deserved punishment, instead he found a belonging, an adoption into God's family through his Son, Jesus. At times Paul used the term 'adoption' instead of sonship, as in Roman culture an adopted person, even if he was formerly a slave, lost all rights and duties to his old family and became a full heir to his new father's estate. As children of God we have become adopted heirs to the promises of God. We may not always feel that way, but the Spirit within us reminds us of who we really are.

Before I received the Holy Spirit I lacked any assurance of my salvation. I felt that I had to respond to every 'altar call' to be given a fresh start! I kept promising God that I would try harder, as he might disown me if I failed to please him. The truth was that I kept messing up my life and felt that I had displeased God. The desire to belong was always there, but it was all too hard for me, as I knew I was incapable of always doing what was right in God's eyes. The Holy Spirit brought revelation to me that it was not about what I had done or even tried to do, but what Jesus had done for me. Once I had become God's child there was no one and nothing that could prevent me from entering into all that God had to offer, except for me! The same is true for every believer.

As a mother of two sons, there is nothing they can do that will alter their status as sons! They may not always do the right thing and there may be times when I would not approve of what they do, as I'm sure that I displeased my own mother on countless occasions! One day they will inherit everything I own, as it is their right as sons.

When God makes a promise it is a surer guarantee than our promises. God has said in his 'will' for his family, that we would be the inheritors of all that Jesus accomplished for us on the cross? Paul knew only too well that it was grace that saved him, turned his life around and enabled him to live devotedly for God. His life was completely redirected but he also realised he had to live according to his new status.

*"For you were once darkness, but now you are light in the Lord. Live as children of the light ---- and find out what pleases the Lord."* Ephesians 5 v 8

We find out what pleases God by reading the bible and developing an intimacy with him. The Word of God illuminates the darkness in us.

Jesus himself said something similar in the Sermon on the Mount: Jesus was and is the 'Light of the World' but the truth is that he has infused his light into us as his sons and daughters. The light only becomes evident as we do his will.

*"You are the light of the world. A town built on a hill cannot be hidden"* Matthew 5 v 14

On my second visit to the Holy Land we arrived in Galilee in the late evening after a long journey from Jerusalem, stopping many times on route. After dinner we walked to the end of the pier by the lake; it was a balmy evening and everything was very still except for the lapping of the water on the shores of the lake. As we looked out into the darkness of the night we saw the town of Tiberius set up high on a hill. It was so brightly lit that it shed its beams across the water and for miles around. Was this similar to what Jesus saw, I wondered? When we know who we are and where we are going; when we feel secure in the arms of a loving God; we too can be lights that reflect the true Light of the World into the darkness of our surroundings, and show the way to those who are lost.

Paul writes to the Christians in Philippi. He reminds them not to grumble and argue, as they were the children of God living among a warped and crooked generation. He said:

*"Then you will shine like stars in the sky as you hold firmly to the word of life."* Philippians 2 v 15

On a clear night it is a beautiful sight to see the stars in all their glory shining brightly and lighting up the universe. Behind it all is a Creator whose name is God the Father and his Son, Jesus Christ sitting at his right hand interceding for us. It is a joyful and precious moment for him to see one of his children stepping out in faith, showing his love and compassion to those who don't yet know him. He longs to enlarge his family.

Only Jesus can fill the emptiness and longings within us. Husbands, wives, parents, children, brothers and sisters can disappoint, but if Jesus becomes the bedrock of our lives, all our other relationships come into focus. We are everlastingly secure in his love as his children, and nothing and no one can persuade us otherwise.

Paul writes to the Christians in Rome;

*"For I am convinced that neither death nor life, neither angels nor demons, neither the present nor the future, nor any powers, neither height nor depth, nor anything else in all creation, will be able to separate us from the love of God that is in Christ Jesus our Lord."* Romans 8 vv 38

(1) God created a woman for Adam
   Genesis 2 vv 18 – 24
(2) Put on the new self! Ephesians 4 v 24
(3) No longer orphans! John 14 v 18
(4) Isaiah 56 v 5 and 62 v 2 & Revelation 3 v12
(5) The Holy Spirit guarantees our inheritance
   Ephesians 1 vv 13-14
(6) The promise of the Holy Spirit
   John 16 vv 6-16 and John 14 v 28

## Something to consider

Have your own experiences of family life been positive or negative? Have you considered that whatever your family or background you can now belong to a new spiritual family?

Being the children of God carries with it special rights and privileges, do you search the scriptures to find out what they are?

The old person you once were should bear no resemblance to the child of God. What has changed for you since you became a Christian?

If you are still living as an 'orphan,' what has to change for you to live as a son or daughter of the living God?

# Afterward

Many people will go to great lengths to hide the black sheep of the family and to cover their past shame, but God brings everything into the light. The bible is the most honest book of all time. God knew that without him in our lives we can end up in the most desperate of situations.

After studying the scriptures and while writing this book, I have tried to immerse myself into the lives of the five women already mentioned and I am persuaded that Jesus was not ashamed of his earthly ancestors. Although some may think that Tamar, Rahab, Ruth, Bathsheba and indeed even Mary were unlikely recipients of God's grace; all of them took great personal risks to fulfil their calling as mothers and in so doing moved from their own brokenness to the beauty of paving the way for a Saviour to be born.

Jesus lived in glory with his Father and the Holy Spirit and had all that he could ever have wanted; yet he chose to become one of us. He was born, not from a line of people with an impeccable pedigree, but from a line of sinners. He risked being thought of as an outsider, a 'nobody,' or even illegitimate, to identify with us and to demonstrate his love for a broken world. He then made the ultimate sacrifice of dying an excruciatingly painful death in our place. He did this so that our lives may be put into the true context of belonging to his family and would take on new meaning and purpose

All too often we live under the heavy burden of shame, guilt and pain – the effects of sin in our lives. It is a wonderfully moving and breath-taking experience to know personal freedom and then to witness others being set free from the chains of their past history. The enemy tries to hold and imprison us with those chains. I stand amazed yet again that all our guilt and shame can be washed away in the river of God's grace and that he is the true healer of broken hearts and lives. We are no longer slaves of the enemy but we can live freely as children of God and heirs with Christ, but we have to accept it as truth and live according to our new status.

*"It was for freedom that Christ set us free. Stand firm, then, and do not let yourselves be burdened again by the yoke of slavery"* Galatians 5 v 1

Paul is encouraging us not to go back to the way we were, but to take our stand in the place God meant for us to be.

Long ago, Charles Wesley in his famous hymn "And can it be?" summed it up so well:

"My chains fell off, my heart was free, I rose went forth and followed thee."

Being religious doesn't cut it, nor even attending church services, but belonging to God's family means having a living, vital and personal relationship with Jesus.

As a mother of sons and now a grandmother, I pray that my children and grandchildren will grow in their knowledge of God and his plan for their lives. I pray too that they will always know the safety, security and intimacy of a loving God and whatever life might hold for them, their hearts would be set free to serve him.

God has painted a picture as it were of us. He speaks of us as being his handiwork or his masterpiece, recreated in his Son to do good works. An artist's masterpiece is the best thing he has ever created. We were so valued that God even planned things for us in advance, before we knew him. Out of the turmoil of our mistakes and failures, we too can move from brokenness to beauty.

God put into operation his rescue plan, which we have seen times without number in the scriptures. The painting of the masterpiece is not yet finished as he adds exquisite touches to our lives day by day. He has much greater plans for us, than we have for ourselves.

God never changes, he is the same yesterday, today and forever and will bring about something good, beautiful and honouring to him, that will not only affect our lives now but also those yet to be born, and for generations to come.

Made in the USA
Charleston, SC
17 March 2015